MONTAUK

nptons International
Film Festival

HAMPTON

NEW YORK

HAMPTONS
PRIVATE

Text by Dan Rattiner

HAMPTONS
PRIVATE

ASSOULINE

INTRODUCTION

During a cold spell about two billion years ago, an enormous glacier slid down from the North Pole, pushing along boulders, sand and tons of other loose debris—until finally the sun warmed the cascading effluvia enough to bring the slide to a slow halt. Soon after, a further warming spell caused the glacier to melt and retreat, leaving behind it a place we now call The Hamptons—part Greenland, part Canada, part Upstate New York and part Connecticut. Along the edge, it meets the sea with a stunning strip of white-sand beach, extending an astonishing forty miles. Because of this beach, The Hamptons is considered one of the most beautiful summer resorts in the world, and it's one of the main reasons why, when I first came as an eager sixteen-year-old, that I decided to spend the rest of my life here.

As my father said at the time, noting the cliffs, the salty sea air, the lakes and ponds, and the rolling moors that populated the long peninsula with a lighthouse at the end, "nobody just winds up here by accident, while drifting through to someplace else. We stick out into the sea. You have to decide to come to The Hamptons. It's a decision." Dad moved our family to The Hamptons because of his love for deep-sea fishing. Meanwhile, it was love at first sight for me as well; and to this day, I cannot imagine living anywhere else.

It is a truly beautiful peninsula. Although just a hundred miles from New York City, eagles still swoop and soar overhead, and whales roll up to the surface to spout. The sea thunders, and the wind whistles. As for the people here, though, it seemed to me that nearly all of them had resolved to settle in

Lifeguards in Montauk.
Previous pages: Striped bass and bluefish abound off the coast of Montauk luring flocks of seagulls.

7

The Hamptons for the very same reason that I did: They had fallen in love; and they had then gone back to the city to tell friends about their find—thus triggering others to follow suit. With that said, a parade of particularly identifiable groups have called The Hamptons home over the years. I've come to think of the arrival of these groups, one after another, somewhat as waves—similar to those of the sea. These waves would sweep over the landscape during several distinct decades; and almost all these new arrivals would stay, overlapping one another, each unique, but settling as a unit, occupying one part of The Hamptons or another, much as the mix of dirt, foliage, sand, boulders and cliffs occupies the various parts of The Hamptons. Thus, they almost all still remain here today—an immense and fascinating patchwork of people and landscapes, coming together as a crazy quilt. Some say it's a match to the patchwork of New York City. But with cows mooing. The city's sixth borough.

The earliest settlers to The Hamptons came in 1640, aboard a small sailboat from Lynn, Massachusetts. They were spurred on by the king of England, who was concerned that since the Dutch had settled Nieu Amsterdam (what would become New York) at the other end of Long Island a hundred miles to the west, he would need an English settlement, a counterweight to the east; and so issued generous grants and other proclamations urging settlers to claim land on the eastern tip of Long Island. These settlers befriended the local Native Americans, and soon produced a series of Old New England towns, of which there were seven, with six miles between each—an hour by buggy—with town ponds, village greens, white Presbyterian churches and broad main streets framed by mighty oaks that remain largely unchanged to this day. Sprinkled among these towns are thirteen cedar-shingled English windmills—forty-foot-tall assemblages with wooden blades that, when fitted with sails, were used to grind grain into flour. Still standing today, they are a stately Hamptons treasure, as well as the largest collection of its kind in America. Not too long ago, one of these mills was occupied by Tennessee Williams, the playwright, who was teaching a class at Southampton College.

These towns were not built down by the ocean. Way back then, because of the rough surf, mist, and damp swamp land just beyond the dunes, it was considered a better idea to build them a mile or so inland, utilizing the space between the town and the beach for farming. The crops planted in the early days included corn, strawberries, potatoes, blueberries, pumpkins, beans and lettuce. Chickens, ducks and cattle were raised. Clams, oysters and mussels came from the bays; bluefish, striped bass and flounder from the sea. The Native Americans taught the settlers how to launch small boats out through the surf to harpoon the whales swimming close to shore; and once towed to the beaches, church bells throughout the town would ring, summoning every able-bodied man down to help drag the beasts up the sand. Fires were started under iron trypots filled with whale blubber, melting it down to oil that would light the town lanterns. Men who failed to come were fined, or even given time in the stocks.

Following the arrival of the first settlers, the next wave of newcomers were members of New York high society, who came to enjoy the summer season shortly after railroad tracks were built out East, in 1863; and the first of this group to arrive was the storied physician Theodore Gaillard Thomas. He traveled with his family, and took up residence in a rooming house, for what he initially believed would be a long weekend. But he was astonished with what he saw—a rural landscape of woods, fields, and ponds, worked by local farmers and clammers who spoke English with an odd, almost unintelligible, working-class English accent. He saw tribes of local Native Americans. He saw the beaches and the cliffs, smelled the salty scent in the air, noted the

crisp temperature—it was July, and about four degrees cooler than in Manhattan—aided by the summer breeze. What a splendid and healthy place this was. He wanted to stay, and for his friends to join him. When he returned to New York, he spoke about The Hamptons with enthusiasm. And thus began the late nineteenth-century wave.

More history of The Hamptons can be found in the old rum-running trails that wind their way through the Hither Woods area of Montauk, at the Marine Museum in Amagansett, and at the Whaling Museum—a unique Sag Harbor facility that celebrates the prosperous years in the 1840s when as many as a hundred whaling ships were tied at Long Wharf.

Beginning in 1919, local charter boat owners would work as rumrunners late at night, motoring out to fetch cases of illegal hooch from ships anchored off of the twelve-mile limit north of the Montauk Lighthouse. They would transport these boxes back to the old bayfront fishing village of Montauk in the wee hours, to pile into trucks headed for

Jesse Joeckel, founder of Whalebone Creative, based in Montauk, and Maggie Malloy take advantage of the famed Hamptons' surf.

11

New York. But Prohibition would end just fourteen years after the practice initially started, in 1933; and the wave of newcomers from this period would eventually do the same—the only wave to do so.

Camp Hero occupies several hundred acres of woods high on a cliff facing the ocean. The well-marked entrance is on the last stretch of the Montauk Parkway, just before the lighthouse. Named for Major General Andrew Hero, a U.S. Army officer who died during World War II, the property consists of the remains of two abandoned military bases. They are, today, partially restored as a historic military park, open to the public. On the eastern end of Camp Hero, huge, sixteen-inch, battleship-sized guns, once outfitted concrete bunkers facing out to sea, to fend off what was expected to be a possible German invasion. The guns could fire a shell sixteen miles. And while no German armada would ever come, after the war, it is said that the booming shells could often still be heard splashing into the sea.

On the other hand, the peculiar remains of Camp Hero have become a cult destination, for people who think that a mind-control and time-travel laboratory was in secret operation on the site during the 1940s and 1950s. Books have been written about it. Films made of it. Some people believe it, or prefer to believe it. Some people don't.

After the army camp closed, the 773rd Radar Squadron was built here, during the Korean War. It was a base consisting of a 123-foot-tall radar tower that, between 1958 and 1963, made a full scan of the skies every 50 seconds, mostly searching for the obvious enemy at the time, the Soviet Union. If missiles were headed toward America, this radar tower would be the first to spot them. A series of underground silos near the county airport in Westhampton could then be opened to reveal a dozen Atlas missiles that, at the push of a button, could be fired back toward Moscow. This was never necessary, however, as the Soviet's missiles never came. The military park is really all that is left of an eighty-year-long history of military activity on the eastern end of Long Island.

When I arrived here, in the mid-twentieth century, I discovered the prospering, oceanfront, high-society summer colony in full bloom. Whitneys, DuPonts, Phipps, Woolworths, Dukes, Fords, Hearsts, Vanderbilts, Hiltons, Chryslers, Murrays, Rockefellers, members of the Morgan, Obelensky and Auchincloss families, all living in grand, ten-room, beachfront "cottages" behind hedgerows and white gates. The thwock of tennis balls and the splash of kids diving into swimming pools dominated the idyllic landscape. Members of this high society were each given a pocket telephone book, called "The Blue Book," on arrival every spring—its pages filled with the names of the other cottage owners in this "summer colony," as they called it, their addresses and phone numbers, the Ivy League schools they went to, and the names of their children. Some entries even included the name of the mansion they occupied. Many houses built between 1890 and 1910 had been given names to pass down to descendants. There were coming out parties, cotillions, weddings and engagement parties. In those days, Jackie Bouvier, the young daughter of "Black Jack" Bouvier, lived at Lasata, a ten-bedroom cottage in East Hampton; and was not only a classic beauty, but also a skilled horsewoman. She would soon marry Jack Kennedy from Hyannis Port and become the First Lady of the United States.

Others had a more wild experience. There was talk back then of "Baby Jane" Holzer, a girl of just nineteen, swinging from a chandelier during a party in Southampton. Scandalous.

Following pages: Arrive to The Hamptons in style behind the wheel of Stuart Parr's 1987 Ferrari Testarossa.

With the arrival of the social set came the private clubs. The Southampton Bathing Corporation, located on a stretch of scenic beach, is a lovely place to sit and enjoy a drink or lunch while watching the waves roll in. There is also the Meadow Club, with beautifully groomed grass tennis courts, and indoor squash courts. Because the rough ocean waves prevented dockage along the ocean beaches, a yacht club had to be created for the high society enclave, on a bay in the Springs, down a country road that wove through farmland and modest homes owned by the locals. Here, behind a private property sign, the Devon Yacht Club docks everything from catboats to sloops to motorboats, to yachts. In addition, there was the Quogue Beach Club, the Shinnecock and National Golf Clubs, the Bath and Tennis Club in Westhampton, the Sebonack Golf Club, and the Quantuck Beach Club.

In the East Hampton circle, members played tennis and golf at the Maidstone Club, which still today features a unique fourteenth hole running parallel to the beach, along a line of sand dunes. If a drive is sliced badly, the ball arcs over the dunes and comes down among the beachgoers on the other side, not far from the rows of club cabanas attended to by waiters. (I have a stubborn slice and on several occasions have unintentionally hit my ball onto the crowded beach; no one was hit in the process, though, just a penalty of stroke and distance.)

The Shinnecock Golf Club is also one of the oldest golf clubs in America. In 1891, William K. Vanderbilt, the grandson of Cornelius, returned from Europe with Willie Dunn, a Scottish golfer, who had taught him the game. Dunn put the ball on a tee near the Shinnecock Indian Reservation, and hit it down through a clearing. Everyone was instantly intrigued. Soon, Dunn, aided by the nearby Native Americans, dug, planted and created the eighteen-hole golf course still being used today.

In 1896, the second U.S. Open was held at the Shinnecock Golf Club, and a young Shinnecock native, seventeen-year-old John Shippen, briefly led at the end of the second day, after special rules were set up to allow him to play as a representative of the club. He is still talked about in the club's history, and remains a local legend. Since then, Shinnecock Golf Club has hosted the U.S. Open an additional four times. In 1995, nineteen-year-old Tiger Woods made his U.S. Open debut. I remember watching from the eighteenth hole as Woods came up the fairway. I was also in the crowd in 2018, when Tiger, arriving by yacht, failed to make the cut, due to a back injury. The U.S. Open is set to return to The Hamptons in 2026.

The Gardiner family has quite the legacy in The Hamptons, dating back to Lion Gardiner in the 1600s, who settled on a private island five square miles in size, sitting two miles off the coast of Amagansett. Several generations and descendants later, Gardiners island was inherited by Robert David Lion Gardiner, the sixteenth lord of the manor, and an acquaintance of mine. One time, sitting on my front deck, he recounted a story about a grandfather clock to illustrate the distinction between the old-money social set and the new-money community. Gardiner's money, however, was even older than old money.

"My chauffeur and I," he told us, "were wrestling a grandfather clock out of the backseat of my car, to take into the Corwin jewelry store in Southampton, to be fixed. It was made by one of the Dominys, an East Hampton clock-making family that lived and worked here back in the eighteenth century. As we crossed the sidewalk, we came upon Mrs. Woolworth. She stopped and raised her glasses to get a better look. 'Oh, Mr. Gardiner—what a lovely clock that is,' she said. 'Wherever did you get it?'"

Following pages: Heidi Klum and kids for *Jane* magazine, 1999. Photographed by Pamela Hanson.

Gardiner sneered back an answer. "We didn't 'get it.' We had it made."

Gardiner hosted me on his island several times. We went out in his yacht, the *Laughing Lady*, flying the skull and crossbones, and spent the day walking around the island. He had hoped to pass along the island to his descendants, but never had children of his own. Gardiner died in 2004; but the two years prior to his passing were spent trying to find someone by the name of Gardiner to be adopted into the family, and, in turn, inherit the land. An attorney in Mississippi was interested in the opportunity for a while, but Gardiner was ultimately unable to convince him. In the end, the island was passed on to his niece, Alexandra Creel Goulet. Perhaps one day, someone down the line bearing the name Gardiner will come along to claim the island.

Soon after high society began to summer in The Hamptons, a great number of artists and writers began to make the move. They lived separately from society's upper crust, and, for the most part, also lived separately from one another. Off in the woods of Southampton, with the soft light streaming in through north-facing studio skylights, Winslow Homer painted; as did Edwin Austin Abbey and William Merritt Chase. The painter Thomas Moran built a turreted mansion in East Hampton, opposite Town Pond. Moran, a bohemian like most artists and writers at the time, traveled to Venice to paint, and brought back with him a full-length Venetian gondola. Every summer, he and his wife, Nimmo, were ferried around Hook Pond in East Hampton by a Venetian gondolier that Moran imported to do the job. In the winter, he kept the gondola on his front lawn for all to see.

In the middle of the twentieth century, the abstract expressionists arrived. Willem de Kooning set up a studio in the rural landscape of the Springs, as did Max Ernst, Franz Kline and Jackson Pollock. Larry Rivers settled in

Southampton, along with Fairfield Porter and Roy Lichtenstein. And Andy Warhol painted in Montauk. There is a place along Springs Fireplace Road in East Hampton, about a half-mile north of the Springs General Store, where you can experience the breathtakingly soft sunlight that these painters found so reminiscent of Provence. It extends for about a mile along that road, and then seems to fade out. The home Jackson Pollock shared with his wife, Lee Krasner, on Springs Fireplace Road is where he made the famous drip paintings. He died at the of age forty-four on that very road, in a drunk-driving accident with two girlfriends as his passengers, while Lee was in Paris.

Painters today seem to congregate in Sag Harbor, a small former whaling town with an old, prewar feel. Working here today are April Gornik, Frank Wimberley, Donald Sultan, Cindy Sherman, Dan Welden, Dan Rizzie, and Eric Fischl. Others including Chuck Close, Julian Schnabel, Ross Bleckner, Jules Feiffer, and Audrey Flack, live in the surrounding Hamptons towns.

Writers began to arrive after World War II, staying at studios in the woods of The Hamptons, where they could write in private. Arthur Miller came with his wife Marilyn Monroe. John Steinbeck wrote three of his books in an octagonal studio he built himself on a backstreet in Sag Harbor—the only town in the area other than Montauk that does not boast seventeenth century New England roots. Edward Albee wrote many plays in a barn in Montauk. Leon Uris wrote in his home off Trout Pond, on Shelter Island. Truman Capote lived here year-round, in a small house amidst the potato fields of Sagaponack. In the same town, was environmentalist, novelist, adventurer, and Buddhist Peter Matthiessen, who established the Ocean Zendo center in the 1980s on his own property, where he welcomed anyone who wanted to meditate. Colson Whitehead wrote about his experience growing up in Sag Harbor's African-American community. Robert Caro

worked on his biographies in a shed in the woods near his home in Sag Harbor. The biographer Walter Isaacson has a home in The Hamptons, as does the literary critic and historian David Reynolds.

On cool evenings, literary giants from the prior generation would congregate at Bobby Van's Tavern in Bridgehampton, where Irwin Shaw, James Jones, George Plimpton, and others, drank, fought and even sang together. Back in the day, next-door at Candy Kitchen, the potato farmers would gather at 7 a.m. to have coffee and discuss that day's potato price, set by the Farm Bureau in Riverhead.

Many world-class photographers have been attracted to the magnificent landscapes of The Hamptons—Gilles Bensimon, Bruce Weber, Richard Avedon, Bert Stern. Bert Morgan became the go-to photographer for the social set in the 1950s; Patrick McMullan in more recent years. Michael Dweck took the well-known photographs in *The End: Montauk, N.Y.*

And then there was Peter Beard who was not only a photographer, but an adventurer.

Beachside Southampton homes are the most sought-after real estate.

He lived in a small cabin on a cliff near the Montauk Lighthouse, and spent decades documenting animals in Africa—even on one occasion bringing an elephant back with him to photograph on his front lawn.

Surfers discovered Montauk in the 1960s. Ditch Plains in Montauk became known around the world for its gentle, rolling surf. It all started in the 1950s, when Sam and Bea Cox moved from Barbados to Montauk, and built the East Deck Motel, protecting the property with a hundred-yard-long jetty sticking out into the sea, along the eastern arc of Ditch Plains. It's this jetty that caused the creation of this sought-after surf just to the west. Today, surfers come breathlessly out of the water, dry off and head to the Ditch Witch food wagon for a healthy treat.

After all that, there came the biggest wave of all—celebrities, movie stars, and billionaires, discovering The Hamptons beginning in the 1980s. The advent of the new-money wave that was so feared by the social set, could be argued to have started with the arrival of Steven Spielberg. But this wave did not truly affect the social set until a man named Barry Trupin, not of a proper religious persuasion, purchased the old, abandoned DuPont mansion, and proceeded to pour more than ten million dollars into reconstruction—money that constructed turrets and spires reminiscent of a French castle. Inside a former library that faced the sea, Trupin erected an entire Irish pub he'd flown from Ireland piece by piece. He also created a glass-enclosed indoor swimming pool for scuba-diving, which he, of course, kept stocked with several sharks. In the end, after a drawn out battle with the social set, Trupin ended up abandoning the overly extravagant chateau, along with the not-quite-finished swimming pool. Years later, it was all torn down by Calvin Klein, who built a steel and glass home for himself.

In a way, the arrival of the new money was a direct result of the descendants of the old money. Younger members of the social set started marrying into new-money families. As far back as the 1930s, Gary Cooper was welcomed at the clubs—the husband of Sandra Shaw. So was actor Clark Gable, and Jack Dempsey, the prize fighter; as was Diana Vreeland and movie star Joan Fontaine.

However it happened, the wave of new money, coming from the worlds of finance, fashion, Broadway, Hollywood, politics, art, literature, and music, is certainly here to stay. Dominating the landscape now are hundreds of five-acre, newly built mansions, in the old social-set style, complete with ten bedrooms, eight bathrooms, and the obligatory swimming pool, tennis courts and gardens sheltered behind hedgerows and white gates. Among those with Hamptons homes are Alec Baldwin, Christie Brinkley, Madonna, Howard Stern, Ron Perelman, Jennifer Lopez, Michael Bloomberg (whose daughter rides in the Hampton Classic Horse Show every Labor Day), Mercedes Ruehl, Lorne Michaels, Martha Stewart, Bill and Hillary Clinton, Paul McCartney, Mel Brooks, Sting, Jon Stewart, Jerry Seinfeld and so many others.

And sure enough, one man built one of the biggest mansions in America here in The Hamptons, some say with money obtained through funds from a magnesium factory in South America. Ira Rennert and his family live on an opulent oceanfront parcel of fifty-nine acres, formerly a Sagaponack potato field, where Rennert constructed more than a dozen buildings in the Italian Renaissance style, with a seventeen-car garage, a playhouse with an antique carousel merry-go-round, a movie house, a religious retreat, a pool house, a gatehouse, several cafés and more. Altogether, the property supports more than 110,000 square feet of buildings. During its construction, writer Kurt Vonnegut, who lived in a colonial saltbox on Main Street in Sagaponack,

announced that he would leave town if this mansion were ever completed. Eight years later, it was finished, albeit hidden behind a newly planted forest of trees, bushes, gardens and long winding driveways—so Vonnegut made the decision to stay.

In 1992, the dire living situation of Jackie Kennedy's aunt and cousin, both named Edith Beale, was discovered. They were found inhabiting a rundown mansion near the ocean in East Hampton, that many had thought was abandoned. The two women—mother and daughter—their twenty-three cats and a racoon, became known across the nation when two filmmakers traversed the jungle of untamed bushes and foliage surrounding the cottage with their cameras. The Beale women shared their story of how they had been left behind when a cruel member of the social set had divorced the mother forty years earlier. The filmmakers, Albert and David Maysles, made the award-winning documentary *Grey Gardens*, which subsequently resulted in a movie starring Jessica Lange and Drew Barrymore, a Broadway musical featuring Christine Ebersole, and several books. Eventually, Jackie, her sister Lee Radziwill and the rest of the Bouvier family came together to fix up the place. Once the mother died, Edith Beale the Younger moved to Palm Beach.

All manner of recreation is available in The Hamptons. There are tennis clubs, beach clubs, golf courses, sandlot softball fields; not to mention the surfcasting, windsurfing, water-skiing, soccer, rugby, ocean-swimming, deep-sea fishing, celebrity-watching, Michelin- and Zagat-starred restaurants, lacrosse and even a minor-league baseball team. Or you can just spend the day shopping in the chic shops along the towns' main streets. Only Sag Harbor is missing these modern-day stores, as the village

St. Andrew's Dune Church in Southampton was built in 1851.

was purposely restored to its former 1930s status, and doesn't allow them. On Saturday afternoons, pop into a gallery along Main Street, to attend an art opening that offers wine and cheese.

A visit to the Walking Dunes in Napeague is the perfect summer-afternoon activity. Climb ninety feet up to the top of the sand dune and enjoy a splendid view of the bay, the ocean, the sunrise and the sunset. The dunes, pushed by the wind, move about three feet a year.

Another special destination is the Big Duck, located on the side of Route 24 in Flanders, northwest of Southampton. Here, a twelve-foot-high and twenty-foot-long white duck made of wood, wire and cement opens into the Big Duck souvenir shop. Originally made as a roadside stand in Riverhead in the 1930s where fresh and roast duck were sold, the Big Duck certainly attracts attention. For a time, when approaching the Big Duck, an AM radio station would recount the origin story of this landmark as told by a breathless Christie Brinkley, the model who now lives in Bridgehampton.

At the Hampton Classic horse show in Bridgehampton, 1993.

Follow the distinct green packaging, and it leads to Tate's Bake Shop on North Sea Road in Southampton, selling fresh-baked chocolate chip and oatmeal raisin cookies. The bake shop started as a cookie stand in 1980, run by the twelve-year-old Kathleen King. People soon fell in love with "Kathleen's Cookies," and when she turned nineteen, she bought the little bakery on North Sea Road. In an unfortunate turn of events, fifteen years later, two of the bakery's accountants schemed to take over the ownership of Kathleen's Cookies. All Kathleen had left was her original Hamptons bakery, a courtesy the accountants allowed—so long as she did not use the Kathleen's Cookies name. As a result, Kathleen, using her old recipe again, began producing her delicious, crowd-pleasing cookies, but this time named after her father Tate (short for potatoes). Eventually, Kathleen would begin selling Tate's Cookies across the nation. Today, Tate's Cookies, still under the direction of Kathleen, are among the best-selling cookies in the world. But that doesn't mean you won't still find her, on occasion, at her original bakeshop pulling out a fresh tray of warm chocolate chip cookies.

The Hamptons has no shortage of classic restaurants—Gosman's, Duryea's and Gurney's in Montauk; Lobster Roll in Napeague; Nick & Toni's and 1770 House in East Hampton; Pierre's, World Pie, Bobby Van's and Topping Rose in Bridgehampton; The American Hotel in Sag Harbor; Shippy's, Sant Ambroeus and The Plaza in Southampton; Edgewater in Hampton Bays; The Patio in Westhampton Beach; The Preston House in Riverhead; North Fork Table in Southold; and Claudio's in Greenport. Multi Aquaculture Systems, in Napeague, is a fish farm and market built on the site of an early twentieth century fish factory where boatloads of bunkers—a small bait fish—were brought, boiled off into paste, packed in barrels and shipped off by rail to New York City glue factories. The complex includes a take-out restaurant with no-nonsense picnic tables.

Or, if preferred, The Hamptons is also a great place to be a home chef. Be your own first settler. Fresh fish and produce are sold at a variety of farm stands, fish markets, wineries, supermarkets, and farmer's markets, offering the bounty of The Hamptons. Recipes from cookbooks written by renowned chefs and food critics living in the local community—Ina Garten, Katie Lee, Florence Fabricant—can help provide inspiration.

For live entertainment, there is the Westhampton Beach Performing Arts Center; Bay Street Theater, in Sag Harbor; and Guild Hall, in East Hampton. The Vail-Leavitt Music Hall, originally a turn-of-the-century opera house in Riverhead, was where Thomas Edison introduced his first, failed attempt at "talking" motion pictures.

The old Parrish Art Museum on Jobs Lane in Southampton built in 1890, has, for years, shown turn-of-the-twentieth century plein air painters, alongside the works of their students. Because many of these paintings today are worth millions of dollars, and have to be stored in a secure and climate-controlled environment, a new Parrish Art Museum was built about two miles away in Water Mill, in order to continue to display these works of art.

Every wave that has come to The Hamptons has left its mark both physically and culturally. Remnants of the social set still abound in The Hamptons, such as the Southampton Hospital benefit, and the Hampton Classic Horse Show—one of the foremost equestrian events in the country—which takes place the week before Labor Day. The rich and famous of The Hamptons come en masse in fancy Easter parade clothes for the grand finale on Labor Day Sunday. The newcomers also have annual can't-miss events, like the hopelessly erotic party and fundraiser at the home of

Following pages: Rolling sand dunes leading to the Atlantic Ocean.

recording artist Ivan Wilzig in Water Mill. Manage to snag an invite and perhaps witness Wilzig dressed as a superhero named Peaceman, the cape-wearing rock star.

The annual Artists-Writers softball game is a contest played on a softball field in East Hampton that has been around for more than a half-century. Many painters and writers play alongside celebrities, athletes and political figures. Bill Clinton has been at two of the games. Carl Bernstein is a regular, as is Mike Lupica and Walter Bernard, the graphic artist.

There is the annual Biggest Clam Contest celebrated in Amagansett at the Marine Museum, and the Fishermen's Fair at Ashawagh Hall in the Springs, where locals and artists mingle—some of whom talk in the Bonac English accent. *Dan's Papers* Kite Fly, on the other hand, is held each August at Sagg Main Beach, while the *Dan's Papers* Taste of Two Forks foodie event offers partygoers samplings from over thirty restaurants and twenty wineries. Meanwhile, every year at the Watermill Center, world-renowned sculptor, performance artist and monument builder Robert Wilson hosts a fantastic art fundraiser, where the students can often be found dressed as woodland creatures up in the trees. Memorial Day and the Fourth of July are also reason to celebrate in The Hamptons, with exuberant and impressive parades and fireworks. The annual Shinnecock Pow Wow takes place over Labor Day Weekend, on the local tribe's reservation, a huge conclave of events, dances, souvenirs, food and drink are offered.

The resort season comes to an end on Columbus Day/Indigenous People's Day weekend, with a four-day-long Hamptons International Film Festival, where movie stars, agents, musicians, script writers and producers meet and exchange information. There are over a hundred films shown across several theatres in the downtowns of the different communities. People from all of these aforementioned waves that have washed over this area—surfers, artists, celebrities, old money, new money, writers, Wall Street, media, locals, politicians, Shinnecocks—wait patiently outside the venues to see the latest independent films vying for prizes.

Winter in The Hamptons is no less festive than the summer months. Two weeks before Christmas, Santa Claus and Mrs. Claus can be seen perched on their sleigh pulled by eight human-sized reindeer, accompanied by elves, clowns and floats during the Saturday morning Santa Parade on Main Street. For the past six years, I have been the one lucky enough to assume the role of East Hampton's jolly Saint Nick—but don't tell that to my kids!

Sometimes, in early January, during that coldest month of the year, I will enjoy a drive out to Camp Hero, and park looking out over the cliff to the rocks on the beach below—the lighthouse picture-perfect just to the east. Offshore to the south, less than a hundred yards away, are several giant boulders that have arrayed themselves into a small island chain—probably something that happened during the last glacier withdrawal. The waves rise and fall enticingly around them. In recent years, dozens of harbor seals from Nova Scotia have begun enjoying this island of rocks as a winter colony. The seals sit there comfortably or swim nearby every year from December to March. The sun shines down upon them. Seagulls swoop. The rocks glisten in the sun. And the seals hoot and honk to one another, perhaps discussing their own recent discovery of The Hamptons.

Following pages: (*left*) The modest group of buildings that comprised Andy Warhol's estate. (*right*) Artist Peter Beard at his home in Montauk, 1981.
Pages 38–39: An oceanfront property included on Andy Warhol's Montauk compound.
Pages 40–41: (*left*) The perfect outdoor Hamptons setup by designer Steven Gambrel in Sag Harbor. (*right*) Collection of paintings on The Hamptons.
Pages 42–43: (*left*) Artist Willem de Kooning in East Hampton, 1953. (*right*) The typical undulating sand fences of The Hamptons.
Pages 44–45: Seagulls spread across an East Hampton beach.

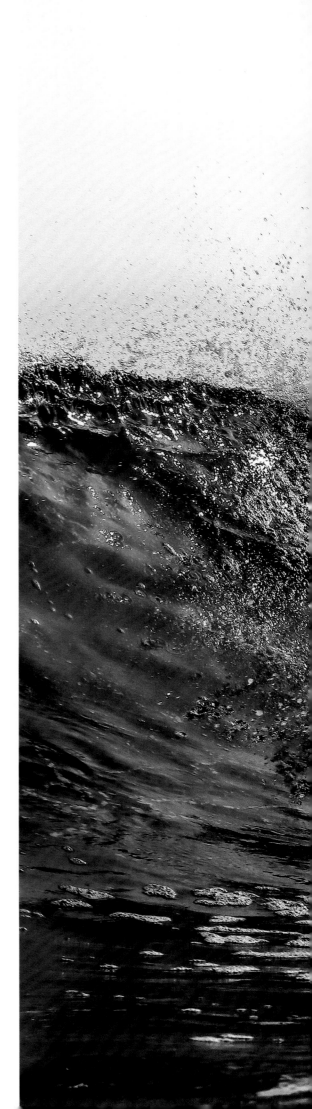

66 [Montauk] is one of those places (where), as soon as you lay your eyes on it, you sort of love it, because it is very raw. And it is just water … You don't have to be in the water, you don't have to see it all the time, but you just feel it here. I love to live in a place where I can feel water. 99

Walter Iooss, *photographer*

66 Montauk will always be my happy place. Being in the water is my own form of meditation. Sometimes, it feels like Hawaii; and there's nothing like escaping to paradise. **99**

Cynthia Rowley, *designer*

"I feel that I belong in Sag Harbor, and I truly believe that the people of the village have accepted us as citizens."

John Steinbeck, *writer*

66 The space, the light, the trees—I just accepted it without thinking about it much. Now I look around with new eyes. I think it's all a kind of miracle. **99**

Willem de Kooning, *artist*

" All the towns along the East End have their own charm, from Southampton to Montauk; and they're close enough that you don't have to pick just one. "

Michael Kors, *designer*

"I always wanted a quiet beachfront home outside the glam, a home that would be restorative and simple to maintain, where I could have privacy, relax and decompress. My home has been my sanctuary."

Kim Cattrall, *actress*

"The Hamptons is where I'm the most truly myself. There is a freedom and an openness. I get to spend time with my family and friends, and I get to live with the beauty of nature—the water, sky, sand, rocks."

Donna Karan, *designer*

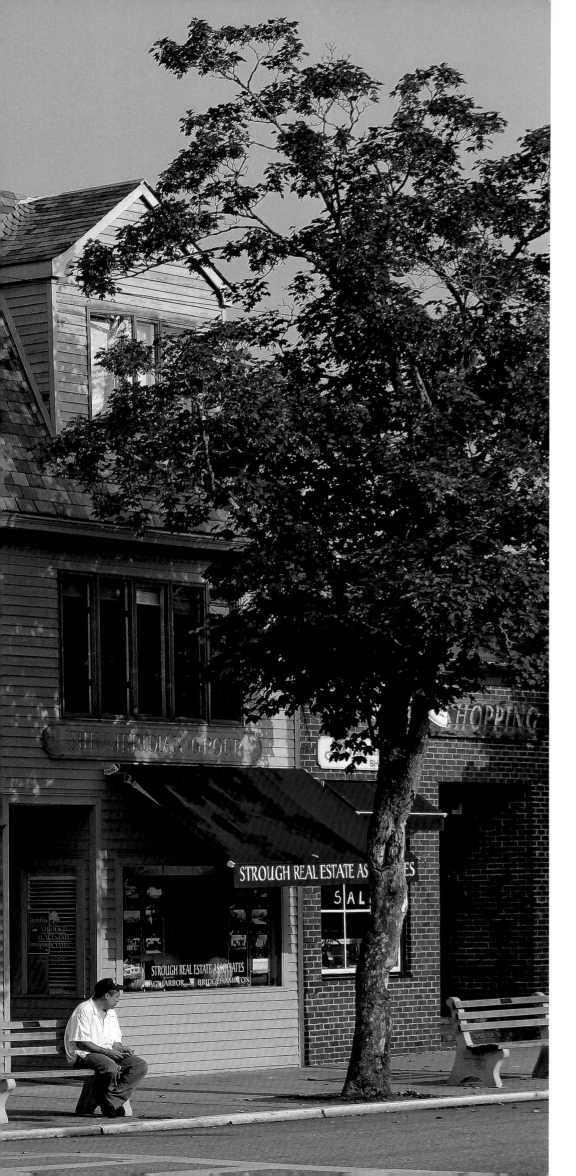

VILLAGE of EAST HAMPTON

C⁰ 1
MAIDSTONE
FIRE DISTRICT

66 The Hamptons have been part of my life with my family for a very long time. I love the ocean, the salty breezes, the rustic shingled cottages, the lighthouses, the special quality of light that drew so many artists here. **99**

Ralph Lauren, *designer*

"I have been coming to The Hamptons since I was born. My hamlet is Southampton, where I learned to ride a bike and swim in the tumultuous Atlantic Ocean—it is part of the fabric of my being. There isn't a day when I am in Southampton that I don't go by the beach. I am a country girl. The Hamptons is a pristine rendition of 'country.'"

Cristina Cuomo, *editor*

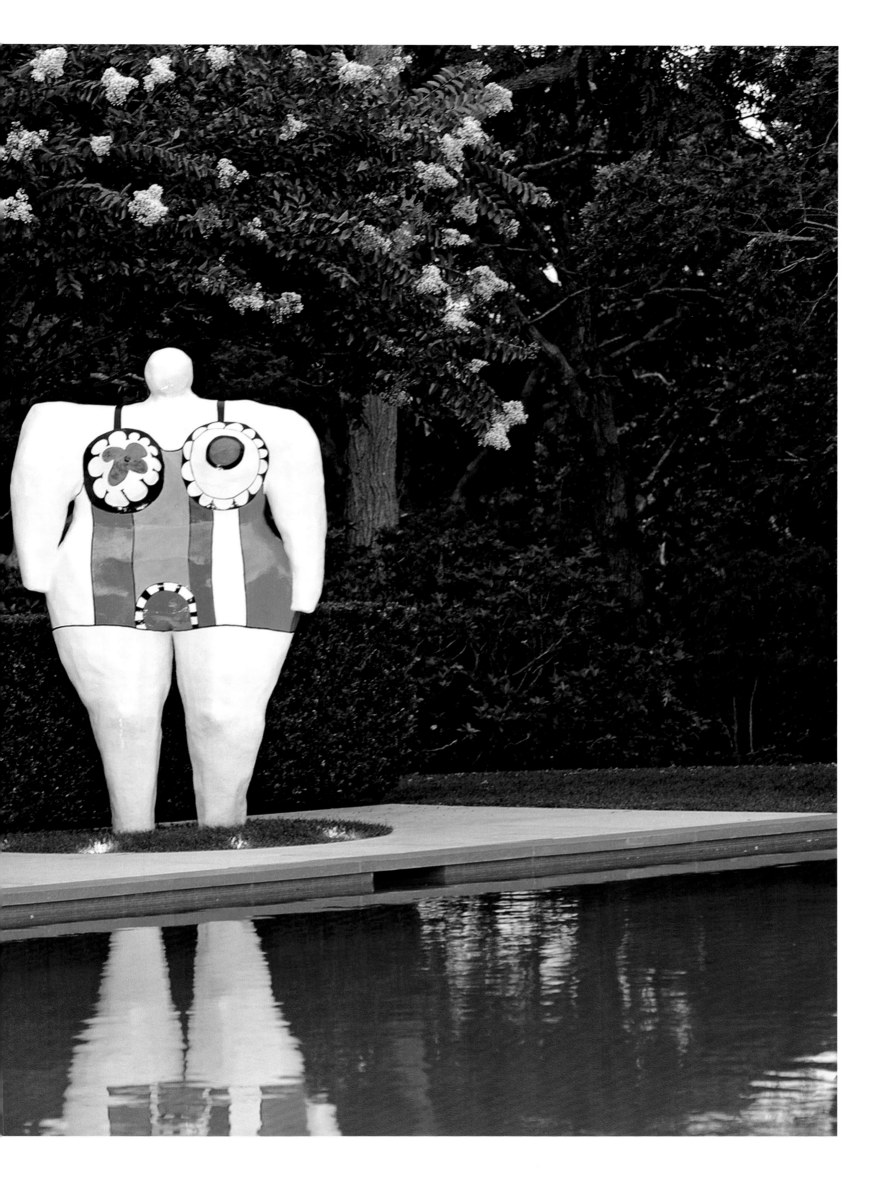

“From Westhampton Beach to Montauk Point, forty miles of history, beauty, culture and fun. No place else like it in the world.”

Bob Colacello, *writer*

"My father was born in Southampton, my mother in East Hampton, and I followed…Back then, The Hamptons were mostly famous for their rural integrity… At least we were lucky enough to have Roy and Dorothy Lichtenstein, Paul Morrissey, Andy Warhol, Willem de Kooning, Larry Rivers, John Chamberlain, and William Wegman with us, for the flavor of artistic authenticity."

Peter Beard, *artist*

"Whenever I get to the dunes and smell the privet and the salt air, I'm anesthetized. It was as if it were calling me to write there."

Christina Haag, *actress*

66 The heart of The Hamptons' boho chic, is the Springs—along the bays, Three Mile Harbor, Fireplace Road and the magical Gerard Drive. Artists, actresses, writers, musicians and the locals—fishermen, gardeners and trades workers—mix at the local farmers market, serenaded by live music. They arrive by pick-up truck in their flip flops to scoop up farm vegetables, fresh breads and fish for Saturday night dinner on their decks. The more carefree you dress (mismatching is de rigeur), the more you fit in. Biking, paddle boarding, fishing, raising chickens, hanging out at the bay beaches and sunset-watching are sports of choice. 99

Christy Ferer, *entrepreneur*

THIS WAY
SEA SLUG
←LOUNGE→

FISH
FARM

"When I first came out to Montauk in the late '70s, it was a sleepy, out-of-the-way, blue-collar town with great surf when it was happening. Years later, it became popular and became part of The Hamptons. I preferred it when it was like Port Aransas, Texas—less people in the water, but I have my old surfing buddies out here, and I have room out in my studio to work and skip all the novelty. I've made most of my paintings here over the last thirty years. I like it here. It's my home."

Julian Schnabel, *artist*

Hamptons
Bohemia

TWO CENTURIES
OF ARTISTS
AND WRITERS
ON THE BEACH

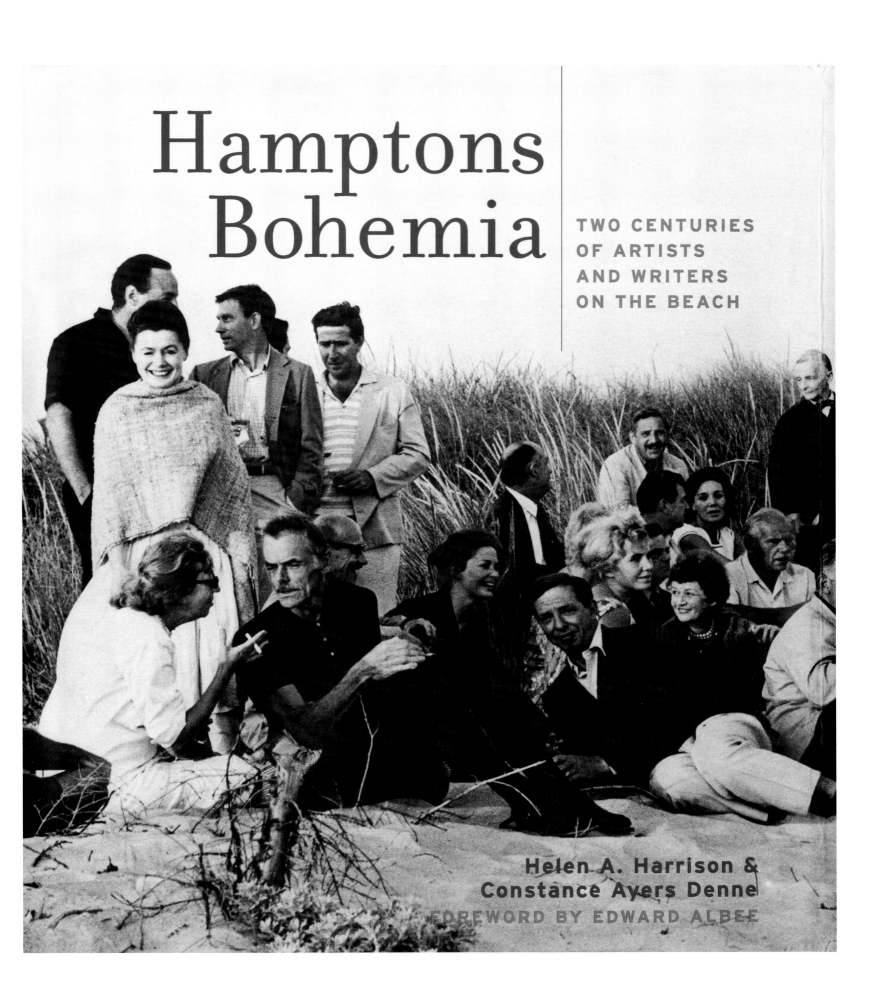

Helen A. Harrison &
Constance Ayers Denne
FOREWORD BY EDWARD ALBEE

"[Andy Warhol] was almost allergic to fresh air, but once in a while felt obliged to leave the city and check in on the happenings at his place in Montauk. Here, a somewhat different person was on display.**"**

Lee Radziwill, *socialite*

"I remember coming here in the early eighties with my family; it was such a magical place at that time. We would wake up early, get pancakes and then head to the beach… and I remember knowing that I always wanted to come back."

Robert McKinley, *designer of The Surf Lodge and Ruschmeyer's*

CAPTIONS

Left: T-shirts for sale on Hot Dog Beach in East Quogue, 1977.

Right: Kathryn Rose Hedges (second from the right) spends the day with friends at the beach in Wainscott, c. 1960.

Beach day in Amagansett.

The Hamptons is known for its serene beaches.

Left: Kate Hudson and Colin Egglesfield on location in Amagansett for the 2011 film *Something Borrowed*.

Right: There is an activity for everyone in The Hamptons, whether it is reading or surfing.

Gurney's Montauk Resort and Seawater Spa opened in the late 1920s.

Jack Nicholson and Diane Keaton in Water Mill filming *Something's Gotta Give* in 2003.

Summertime in Sagaponack.

Designer Ralph Lauren and his wife, Ricky, with their children, David, Andrew and Dylan, drive in a jeep on the beach in East Hampton, 1977.

Left: The Bridgehampton Inn has been owned and operated by Sybille van Kempen for over two decades.

Right: A quintessential summer scene in The Hamptons. Photographed by Melanie Acevedo.

Designer and artist Rogan Gregory, Jason Engdahl and Patrick Zung participate in a "teepee-off" at The Surf Lodge in Montauk.

Picnic in Amagansett. Photographed by Pamela Hanson.

Left: Surf-casting fishermen working the shore near the historic Montauk Point lighthouse, 1939.

Right: Photographer Bruce Weber attends the Sixteenth Annual Rell Sunn Surf Contest Benefit at Ditch Plains in 2014.

Catching a wave in Montauk.

Left: Lauren Morgan Roscopf stops at Lunch for their beloved lobster roll.

Right: A snack from the Montaco food truck after a day of surfing.

Left: A Hamptons picnic always includes an ocean view.

Right: Wood-fired pizza from Moby's in East Hampton.

Sylvester Manor Farm to Table dinner event on Shelter Island, 2014.

Surf-casters in Montauk.

Robert D. L. Gardiner leads *The Laughing Lady*, his 1930s Luders speedboat, away from Gardiners Island in the late 1990s.

Left: Boats off the coast of Sag Harbor.

Right: Ariana Jasuta, wearing a Summer Label swimsuit, cools off on a hot summer day at Liar's Saloon.

Docks at Sag Harbor.

The Sag Harbor marina is full of luxury yachts, including Ted Conklin's *America*.

Chartering a yacht for the day is a must-try Hamptons activity.

Left: Morning coffee at Baron's Cove.

Right: Breakwater Yacht Club in The Hamptons.

Sag Harbor's Harborfest features the annual Whaleboat Races.

The annual Hamptons Paddle for Pink event to benefit the Breast Cancer Research Foundation, 2019.

Guests in The Hamptons include Kelly Bensimon, Delfina Blaquier, Nicky and Charlie Klarsfeld, Antonella Bertello, Rakiem Walker, Sabrina Burda and Noelle Pallais, Iris Zonlight, King Harris, Doris Castells, John Paulson, Edgar Bohlen, and Miss Trish of Capri.

Sag Harbor marina, with Billy Joel's house in the lower-left foreground.

Left: Sunset Beach Hotel on Shelter Island.

Right: Andrew Cogan's home on Shelter Island, designed by Michael Haverland.

Cedar-shingled Amagansett home.

Director Henry Jaglom on the set of *Last Summer in the Hamptons*, in 1995.

Nacho Figueras with his Ferrari at his home in Bridgehampton, 2010.

Lisa Perry's Hamptons estate, built in the early 1900s by architect and landscape designer Guy Lowell, is located in a secluded part of North Haven.

Outdoor dining setup at Lisa Perry's Hamptons home.

Genius Loci home in Montauk, by Bates Masi + Architects.

Peter Cohen's house in East Hampton, designed by Norman Jaffe, 1982.

Shirley Held, wife of author Joseph Heller, in the garden of her East Hampton home, 1979.

Eunice Bailey Oakes Gardiner and husband Robert David Lion Gardiner picnic with guests on Gardiners Island, 1968.

Ron Perelman's Georgica Pond Estate in East Hampton.

American socialite Anne McDonnell Ford and her new husband, automobile executive Henry Ford II, on the lawn of Anne's family's house, after their wedding in Southampton, 1940.

Happy guest at a Hamptons social gathering.

Truman Capote in his Jaguar XKE at his Sagaponack beach house, as seen in *Vogue*, 1965.

Left: Venus Williams attends the EleVen by Venus Williams party in Southampton, 2012.

Right: Sitting area of the tennis court at Christy Ferer's East Hampton home.

The home of J. Christopher Burch in Southampton.

English gardens at The Baker House 1650 in East Hampton.

The many shades of green in The Hamptons.

Shelter Island pool house, designed by General Assembly.

Erika Bearman's Hamptons home, designed by Miles Redd, is set against luscious greenery.

Moet Hennessy's Volcan De Mi Tierra Batch 1 Dinner, in Amagansett, 2017.

A picturesque sitting area at Solé East Hotel in Montauk.

Left: A benefit held at Quail Hill Farm, in Amagansett, 2010.

Right: John Steinbeck's summer home in Sag Harbor, 1961.

Rosewood is a large horse farm in The Hamptons, full of joy, warmth and a tasteful European lifestyle.

Left: Northwest Peach Farm residence in East Hampton, designed by Bates Masi + Architects.

Right: Designer Elie Tahari's Southampton home.

Initially built as a hunting lodge in Southampton on the Rogers Estate, this mansion was transformed into a social club called the "Port of Missing Men," 1937.

The Maidstone Hotel in East Hampton.

Left: Studio Robert McKinley transformed a 1970s, ranch-style home in Montauk, to create the McKinley Bungalow Fairview.

Right: Baron's Cove Hotel in Sag Harbor is a home away from home.

The Hamptons is known for its verdant gardens.

Serena and Lily bikes, provided by A Room at the Beach Hotel, are the ideal Hamptons transportation.

Left: Redwoods tower over the grounds of A Room at the Beach Hotel, in Bridgehampton.

Right: The perfect reading spot.

Nina Agdal, for *Hamptons Magazine*.

Left: North Sea residence in Southampton, designed by Shelton Mindel.

Right: The barn at Rosewood.

The Palm at the Huntting Inn, in East Hampton.

The American Hotel on Main Street, in Sag Harbor.

Shops on Main Street in East Hampton.

Left: 75 Main restaurant in Southampton.

Right: A day of shopping in The Hamptons.

Main Street in Sag Harbor.

Left: Camilla Priest on a bike-ride along the Hamptons dunes.

Right: The American Hotel dining porch in Sag Harbor.

Jean Georges at Topping Rose House in Bridgehampton.

In The Hamptons, people take advantage of the great weather and numerous outdoor activities.

Ralph Lauren store on Main Street in East Hampton.

RJ King and Theo Battaglia at the Oliver Peoples event at The Surf Lodge, 2017.

Joanna Nanci, a surfer from Amagansett, at Ditch Plains beach.

Car racing in Bridgehampton, 1960.

Maaike Klaasen models the latest fashions in The Hamptons.

Spectators watch the Mercedes-Benz Polo Challenge in Bridgehampton, 2001.

Left: Beyoncé and Jay-Z driving with the top down in The Hamptons.

Right: Taylor Antrim's home on Shelter Island.

Left: East Hampton pool deck.

Right: Hillary Bone and Annabel Schwartz hanging by the pool in The Hamptons.

Dinner with Jackson Pollock event at Lisa Perry's home in Sag Harbor, featuring a sculpture by Niki de Saint Phalle.

American painter and jazz musician Larry Rivers plays the saxophone with an ensemble in The Hamptons, 1984.

Dan Bailey and Lauren Chu at an event in Sag Harbor, 2016.

Tyson Beckford at The Surf Lodge, in Montauk, 2008.

Barbara Palvin, photographed in The Hamptons for *Harper's Bazaar*.

Stuart Parr's Clearhouse, on Shelter Island.

Bustling Sag Harbor Bay.

Maidstone Golf Club in East Hampton.

The 118th U.S. Open Championship at the Shinnecock Hills Golf Club in Southampton, 2018.

Left: Hamptons author and caddy Scott Werner.

Right: Christie Brinkley during the 25th Annual Artists-Writers Softball Game in East Hampton, 1989.

Hampton league baseball game between the Sag Harbor Whalers and the Riverhead Tomcats at Mashashimuet Park, 2009.

The 1770 House Restaurant and Inn on Main Street in East Hampton.

Four competitors pose at the Hampton Classic Horse Show in Bridgehampton.

Polo star Nacho Figueras rests on the sidelines after a match in Bridgehampton, 2007.

Polo players attend the awards ceremony at the 1999 Mercedes-Benz Polo Challenge, held in Bridgehampton.

Left: A game of croquet at the DETAILS and Jack Purcell event in Sag Harbor, 2010.

Right: Patrick Foy competes in a croquet tournament at The Meadow Club, in Southampton, 2007.

Deer hide amongst the bushes in The Hamptons.

Corn maze in Bridgehampton.

Scott Chaskey, manager of Quail Hill Farm, helps to harvest tomatoes at the farm in Amagansett, 2008.

Wölffer Estate Vineyard has been producing wine and cider in Sagaponack since 1988.

Paul Hamilton, a Montauk farmer, and his son Walker show off a basket of produce picked from a garden in East Hampton.

Tree-lined Southampton street.

Left: The vibrant colors of fall in The Hamptons.

Right: Mickey and Peggy Drexler's dogs enjoy the autumn weather.

Christie Brinkley at her Southampton home.

Kelly Connor takes a Chevy Impala for a spin on Shelter Island.

Lobsterman Al Schaeffer prepares his boat, *Leatherneck*, at the dock in Montauk.

The Sag Harbor windmill.

Left: Woven steel wall sculpture by Eric Gushee at the Good Design Hamptons store.

Right: An early eighteenth century Dutch barn in East Hampton in the process of being rebuilt.

Parrish Art Museum in Water Mill.

Left: Artist Bradley Theodore attends an event at Fairview Farm at Mecox in Bridgehampton, 2015.

Right: Wayne Coyne, from The Flaming Lips, at The Surf Lodge, 2015.

Scenes from the Springs, featuring Christy Ferer, Kim Cattrall, Jenni Muldaur, Cindy Sherman, Edwina von Gal, Anh Duong, Pamela Hanson and Lucy Winton.

Left: The Fish Farm in Amagansett.

Right: Cindy Sherman and Christy Ferer fishing off the coast of Shelter Island.

Artist Roy Lichtenstein in his Southampton studio, 1977.

Left: Andy Warhol filming in Montauk, 1960s.

Right: Artworks by Costantino Nivola, Michael Lekakis and Ernest Briggs on display at the Eric Firestone Gallery in East Hampton, 2019.

Luxury Hamptons hotel Gurney's Montauk Resort and Seawater Spa is located right on the beach.

Painter Jackson Pollock and his wife, Lee Krasner, in his studio at the Springs, East Hampton, 1953.

Untitled, self portrait of Julian Schnabel with his dog Tina at his Montauk studio, 2004. 24 x 20 inch color Polaroid.

Left: *15.08.18 #6 Ruby-Mike*, by Joni Sternbach. Montauk, 2015.

Right: *Hamptons Bohemia: Two Centuries of Artists and Writers on the Beach*, by Helen A. Harrison.

The rugged Montauk landscape.

Andy Warhol filming with his friend Lee Radziwill, in Montauk, 1972.

Winter swim in the turtle cove at Montauk Point, with a view of the Montauk Lighthouse.

Lifeguards, surfers and paddleboarders line up for a photo before an annual charity swim in East Hampton, 2007.

Left: Nautical bar area of Navy Beach restaurant, in Montauk.

Right: Hamptons home of interior designer Richard Mishaan.

The Surf Lodge is a boho-chic hotel and restaurant in Montauk.

Left: A view of Fort Pond Bay from Navy Beach.

Right: The bluffs of Old Montauk Highway are known as The Seven Sisters, named after the original homes built there, owned by Andy Warhol, Peter Beard, Dick Cavett, Richard Avedon and Paul Simon.

Post-surf shower in Amagansett.

Left: John Steinbeck in Sag Harbor, c. 1962.

Right: Boutiques on Jobs Lane, in Southampton.

Left: Quaint detail on a Hamptons home.

Right: It is always a good day to fish in The Hamptons.

Lola Kirke, Lili Chemla, Elizabeth Sonnenberg and Jenny Sonnenberg in the hot tub. Photographed by Pamela Hanson.

Waterfront rooms at Gurney's Star Island Resort and Marina.

Sam Shafian (right) relaxes at The Surf Lodge, in Montauk, 2008.

Sag Harbor dock at sunset.

ACKNOWLEDGMENTS

The author would like to thank the following: Chris Wasserstein; Rhone Baker; Adelaide de Menil; Alec Baldwin; Billy Joel; Kim Parrott; Amy Zerner; Nancy Premisler; Avery Corman; Ben Wasserstein; Maya Baker; Len Riggio; Bill Hattrick; Jesse Warren; Al Franken; Masha Udensiva; Bill O'Reilly; Bonnie Cannon; Solange Baker; Carl Bernstein; Mercedes Ruehl; Mark Chapman; Caroline Hirsch; Christie Brinkley; David Lion Rattiner; Costas Kondylis; Eric Woodward; Victoria Schneps; Dariele Watnick; Pamela Wasserstein; Bob Caro; Elizabeth White-Fricker; Paul Jeffers; Dennis Suskind; Lance Gumbs; Eddie Burke Sr.; Elsie Chandler; Martha Stewart; Fred Thiele; Goeff Lynch; Hans Van de Bovenkamp; Lou Meisel; Adam Shapiro; Kate Wasserstein; Henry Hildreth; Henry Uihlein; Shirley Strum Kenny; Edward Burke Jr.; Susyn Reeve; Wilbur Ross; Scoop Wasserstein; Jack Lenor Larsen; Deb McEneaney; Walter Isaacson; Jerry Della Femina; Jimmy Finkelstein; Joan Baker; Liz Parrott; Rudy Gaskins; Joan Hamburg; Joan Zandell; Jules Feiffer; Chuck Scarborough; Mack Parrott; Kathy Parrott; John Catsimatides; Pamela Topham; Toni Ross; Juliet Papa; Courtney Sale Ross; Karl Grossman; Kacee Fried; Kaylie Jones; Kim Cattrall; Mark Levinson; James Peltz; Mark Petering; Ken Lipper; Ken Auletta; Kimberly Goff; Kristen Nyitray; Scott Miller; Lucy Jane Wasserstein; Julia Turner; Adam Rattiner; Michael Premisler; Maria Savage; Mark Epley; Marty Shepard; Judy Shepard; Mark Larner; Alena Rattiner; Sophia Madison Rattiner; Mike Lupica; Eli Shapiro; Gabriel Rattiner; Monte Farber; Natasha Udensiva Brenner; Mischa Brenner; Liza Fiore; Paul Brennan; Nejma Khanum Beard; Pia Lindstrom; Richard Weise; Cecil Hoge; Owen Wasserstein; Ron Delsener; Pele; Bill Clinton; Steve Tanger; Stewart Lane; Susan Isaacs; Sherri Larner; Suzanne O'Malley; Tom Clavin; Tony Hitchcock; Valerie Heller; Walter Bernard; Michael Paraskevas; William Pickens III; Roger Rosenblatt; Dick Cavett; Jimmy Buffet; Arthur Shapiro; Father Alex; Mel Brooks; Mr. G.; Ted Conklin; Adrian Cohen; Derek Enlander; Stephanie Parrot; Steven Spielberg; Helen Harrison; April Gornik; Jay Schneiderman; Ruby Jackson; Kevin Baker; Jerry Cohen; Bob Edelman; Joan Jedell; Joanna Barr; David Reynolds; Kathy Rae; Daniel Simone; Adelia Powell; Marie Villas; Eric Cohen; Lee Meyer; Dave Barr; Edith Seligson; Joyce Menschel; Adele Fuchsberg; Steven Gaines.

Assouline would like to thank the following people for their contributions to this book: Barbara von Bismarck, Delfina Blaquier, Bob Colacello, Christy Ferer, Pamela Hanson, Cristina Macaya, Noelle Pallais, Lisa Perry, Julian Schnabel and Rakiem Walker.

The publisher would also like to thank the following people: Lauren Morgan Roscopf, A Lo Profile; Lucy Swift Weber, A Room at the Beach; Nina Agdal; Susan Lennon, Alamy Stock Photo; Matt Albiani; Glen Allsop; Antoine Verglas, Lera Loeb, Antoine Verglas Studio; David Morales Jr., Aperture Talent Agency; Michael Van Horne, Art + Commerce; Stefanie Breslin, Art Partner; Jennifer Belt, Ken Johnston, Art Resource; Laura Lapitino, Battalion PR; Kelly Killoren Bensimon; Connor Norton, BFA; Sybille van Kempen, Bridgehampton Inn; Thomas Haggerty, Bridgeman Images; Kyril Bromley; Wilson Taylor, Camron PR; Jessica Orlowicz, Cape Resorts; Leigh Grissom, Center for Creative Photography; Lili Chemla; Stephanie Clark; Jamie Lee, Tiffany Boodram, Condé Nast Licensing; Kelly Connor; Courtney Daniels; Jenny M. Quinn, DC&CO Studios; Ted Delano; Mikey DeTemple; Danielle Gingerich, DG Creative; Rob Magnotta, Edge Reps; Kara Winters, Eric Firestone Gallery; Jessica Alper, Factory PR; Nacho Figueras; Joe Fletcher; Milan Blagojevic, Full Picture; Didier Gault; Brian Stehlin, Getty Images; Durell Godfrey; Gordon M. Grant; Brigid Cotter, Gurney's Resorts; Martin Haake; Lizzie Wells, Hamptons Social; Conor Harrigan; Michael Heller; Debby Hymowitz; Timea Szecsi, Icon Model Management; James Katsipis; Kelli Delaney, KDHamptons; Leah Herman, Kindred Co.; Lola Kirke; Mark Kopko; Kate Kuhner; Evan R. Kulman; Doug Kuntz; Robyn Lea; Michael Shulman, MAGNUM Photos; Kimberly Ayl, Massif Management; Michael Del Piero, Judson Barrett-O'Keefe, Michael Del Piero Good Design Hamptons; Moby's; Malin Hedblom, Mordecai AB; Leyla Marchetto, Navy Beach Restaurant; Tony Vavroch, NY Model Management; Melissa LeBoeuf, OTTO Archive; Liz Andrien, Pamela Hanson Inc.; Mo Karadag, Paparazzi Model Management; Fran Parente; John Power; Camilla Priest; Chloe J. Rajs; Omar Ramos; Heather Rose Rauscher; Pip Chodorov, Re:Voir; Holly Lowman, Red Light Management; Ines Rivero; Crystal Henry, Redux Pictures; Annabel Schwartz; Vincent Mounier, Shutterstock; Daniel Tucker, Sideshow Media; Dave Ceva, Solé East Hotel; Jenny and Elizabeth Sonnenberg; Tina Dellamonica, Splash; Joni Sternbach; Eric Striffler; Stuart Parr, Gregory Johnston, Stuart Parr Design; Studio Robert McKinley; Suzee Foster, The 1770 House; Antonella Bertello, The Baker House 1650; The Maidstone; The Surf Lodge; Samantha Voutsinas, Topping Rose House; Anthony Tran, Trunk Archive; Ariana Jasuta, TRVL Collective; Laine Turner; Meghan Gilmore, Willy Social; Valerie Fraser, Wölffer Estate Vineyard; Capt. Shannon Carleton, Yacht Kelpie.

CREDITS

Pp. 4-5: Tosh Brown/Alamy Stock Photo; pp. 6, 174-175: Michael Dwyer/Alamy Stock Photo; pp. 10-11: Karsten Moran/The New York Times/Redux; pp. 14-15: Glen Allsop/Stuart Parr Collection; pp. 18-19, 66-67, 176, 294-295: © Pamela Hanson; pp. 22-23, 44-45, 129, 134-135, 147, 165, 240-241, 242, 243, 292, 293: © Martine Assouline; p. 26: Mark Kopko Photography; pp. 28-29, 226-227: Mark Peterson/Corbis/Getty Images; pp. 32-33: Karen Foley Photography/Getty Images; pp. 36, 80-81, 86-87, 114-115, 120-121, 216: © Doug Kuntz; pp. 37, 217: Ron Galella/Ron Galella Collection/Getty Images; pp. 38-39, 183: © Assouline; p. 40: Eric Piasecki/OTTO; p. 41: Adrian Gaut/Trunk Archive; p. 42: Tony Vaccaro/Bridgeman Images; p. 43: Nikola Bradonjic/Stocksy; p. 46: Dan Neville/Newsday RM/Getty Images; p. 47: Courtesy of Granddaughter Heather Rose Rauscher; pp. 48-49: Martine Franck/Magnum Photos; pp. 50-51, 82, 98-99, 210-211: Gavin Zeigler/Alamy Stock Photo; p. 52: Bobby Bank/WireImage/Getty Images; pp. 53, 231: © Durell Godfrey; pp. 54-55, 266-267, 296-297: Courtesy of Gurney's Resorts; pp. 56-57: TCD/Prod.DB/Alamy Stock Photo; pp. 58-59: Kasia Wandycz/Paris Match/Getty Images; pp. 60-61, 116-117, 200-201: Susan Wood/Getty Images; p. 62: Photography: Conor Harrigan; p. 63: Melanie Acevedo/Trunk Archive; pp. 64-65: Kelly Shimoda/Redux; pp. 68, 118-119: Alfred Eisenstaedt/The LIFE Picture Collection/Getty Images; p. 69: John Lamparski/Getty Images; pp. 70-71: © John Power; p. 72: Lauren Morgan Roscopf; p. 73: Ben Watts/Trunk Archive; pp. 74, 91: Photography by Eric Striffler; p. 75: Courtesy of Moby's/Photography by Erica Gannett; pp. 76-77: Angela Pham/BFA.com; pp. 78-79, 107, 144, 170-171, 218-219, 224-225, 229, 232-233, 234-235, 248-249, 291, 298-299: © Gordon M. Grant; p. 83: Courtesy of Ariana Jasuta/Photography by Brent Davis; pp. 84-85: manjagui/Shutterstock; pp. 88-89: Courtesy of Yacht Kelpie; pp. 90, 155: Courtesy of Cape Resorts; pp. 92-93: Michael Heller/The Sag Harbor Express; pp. 94-95, 128: Sonia Moskowitz/Getty Images; p. 96 (clockwise from top left): Courtesy of The Golden Pear; © Matt Albiani; Courtesy of Delfina Blaquier; Courtesy of Rakiem Walker; © Jake Rajs; © Pamela Hanson; Photography: Daniel D'Ottavio/Courtesy of The Baker House 1650; Photographer: Sandra Arenas; p. 97: Photographer: Christophe von Hohenberg; p. 100: Matthew Hranek/Art + Commerce; p. 101: Roger Davies/OTTO; pp. 102-103: Trevor Tondro/OTTO; pp. 104-105: Michael Ochs Archives/Getty Images; pp. 108-109, 110-111: © Robyn Lea; pp. 112-113, 148, 164: Michael Moran/OTTO; pp. 122-123: Morgan Collection/Getty Images; pp. 124-125: Jessica Craig-Martin/Trunk Archive; pp. 126-127: Horst P. Horst/Conde Nast/Getty Images; pp. 130-131, 139: William Waldron/OTTO; p. 132: Photography: Daniel D'Ottavio/Courtesy of The Baker House 1650; p. 133: Photography: Yuxi Liu/Courtesy of The Baker House 1650; pp. 136-137: Joe Fletcher; pp. 140-141: Joe Schildhorn/BFA.com; pp. 142-143: Aaron Katowski/Courtesy of Solé East Hotel; p. 145: Max Heine/Newsday RM/Getty Images; p. 146: (top left, bottom right) © Martine Assouline; (top right) Courtesy of Cristina Macaya; (middle row, bottom left) Courtesy of Barbara von Bismarck; p. 149: Douglas Friedman/Trunk Archive; pp. 150-151: The Museum of the City of New York/Art Resource, NY; pp. 152-153: Fran Parente; pp. 154, 196: Photography: Nicole Franzen; pp. 156-157: © Jake Rajs 2012; pp. 158-159, 160, 161: Photography by Sasha Lytvyn/Courtesy of A Room at the Beach; p. 163: © Antoine Verglas; pp. 166-167: Photography by Lizzie Wells/Courtesy of Hamptons Social; pp. 168-169: Russell Kord/Alamy Stock Photo; p. 172: Ian G Dagnall/Alamy Stock Photo; p. 173: Photo by Kelli Delaney of KDHamptons; p. 177: Stephen Saks Photography/Alamy Stock Photo; pp. 178-179: Jenna Gallo Photography; p. 180: © Prosper Assouline, except: (top left) Courtesy of Christy Ferer; (bottom left) Photography: Didier Gault/Model: Ines Rivero; p. 181: © Prosper Assouline, except: (top left) Kasia Wandycz/Paris Match/Getty Images; (top right) Danil Nevsky/Stocksy; (right column, black and white) Elizabeth Kuhner Archive; (bottom left) © Martine Assouline; pp. 184-185: Carl Timpone/BFA.com; pp. 186-187: Jason Andrew/The New York Times/Redux; pp. 188-189: Joe Scherschel/The LIFE Picture Collection/Getty Images; p. 191: © Danny Cardozo, @decostudios, @dannycardozo; pp. 192-193: Spencer Platt/Getty Images; p. 194: © Splash; p. 195: Christopher Sturman/Trunk Archive; p. 197: Courtesy of Annabel Schwartz; pp. 198-199: Hunter Abrams/BFA.com; pp. 202-203: David X Prutting/BFA.com; pp. 204-205, 228: Nick Hunt/Patrick McMullan/Getty Images; p. 207: Terry Richardson/Art Partner; pp. 208-209: Clearhouse Stuart Parr Design/Photography: Bill Timmerman; pp. 212-213: Kyril Bromley; pp. 214-215: Koji Aoki/AFLO Sport/Alamy Live News; pp. 220-221: Jacques LeBlanc for The 1770 House; pp. 222-223: © Debby Hymowitz; pp. 236-237: Mark Weinberg/Wölffer Estate Vineyard; pp. 238-239: Daniel Gonzalez/The New York Times/Redux; pp. 244-245: Karin Kohlberg/Contour/Getty Images; pp. 246-247: Marko MacPherson/Vogue © Conde Nast; p. 251: Omniphoto/UIG/Bridgeman Images; pp. 252, 253: Photographed by Lukas Machnik/Courtesy of Michael Del Piero Good Design Hamptons; pp. 254-255: Hufton-Crow-VIEW/Alamy Stock Photo; p. 256: Madison McGaw/BFA.com; p. 257: Kelly Taub/BFA.com; pp. 259, 260, 261: Courtesy of Christy Ferer; pp. 262-263: Bettmann/Getty Images; p. 264: The Billy Name Estate/Art Resource, NY; p. 265: Courtesy of Eric Firestone Gallery; pp. 268-269: Tony Vaccaro/Getty Images; pp. 270-271: Photograph by Julian Schnabel; p. 272: © Joni Sternbach; p. 273: © 1991 Hans Namuth Estate, Courtesy Center for Creative Photography; pp. 274-275: Kirill Orlov/Stocksy; p. 276: © Jonas Mekas; pp. 278-279: © James Katsipis; pp. 280-281: Robert Nickelsberg/Getty Images; pp. 282, 286: Photography by Noah Fecks/Courtesy of Navy Beach; p. 283: Ty Cole/OTTO; p. 285: Photography by StayMarquis/Courtesy of The Surf Lodge; p. 287: Mikey DeTemple/Massif; pp. 288-289: Johnny Miller/Edge Reps; p. 290: Rolls Press/Popperfoto/Getty Images; pp. 300-301: Tana Lee Alves/WireImage/Getty Images.

Every possible effort has been made to identify and contact all rights holders and obtain their permission for work appearing in these pages. Any errors or omissions brought to the publisher's attention will be corrected in future editions.

Assouline supports *One Tree Planted* in its commitment to create a more sustainable world through reforestation.

Front cover design © Martine Assouline.
Back cover tip-on (clockwise from top left):
Michael Dwyer/Alamy Stock Photo; © Martine Assouline; Courtesy of Delfina Blaquier; © Doug Kuntz.
Endpages: © Martin Haake.

© 2021 Assouline Publishing
3 Park Avenue, 27th floor
New York, NY 10016 USA
Tel: 212-989-6769 Fax: 212-647-0005
assouline.com

Printed in Italy by Grafiche Milani.
ISBN: 9781614289876

INTERNATIO
FLUGPOST
USSTELLU
POSTA   12:2
WI
STAD
WIEN

SAG HARBOR

EA

BRIDGEHAMPTON

WATER MILL

ATLANTIC
OCEAN

SOUTHAMPTON